WOW HITS 2015

SONGBOOK

INCLUDES 3 BONUS SONGS!

33 OF TODAY'S TOP CHRISTIAN ARTISTS & HITS

ALSO AVAILABLE **WOW HITS 2015** CD
Standard #602537509744 • Deluxe Edition #602537509836

Transcribed and Engraved by
DAVID THIBODEAUX

Edited by
KATHY McMANUS & ANISSA SANBORN

Art Production by
FUDGE CREATIVE

For digital availability of this and other products, go to *wordmusic.com*

ALSO AVAILABLE FROM WOW HITS 2015 DELUXE EDITION:
DOWNLOADABLE AT WORDMUSIC.COM

LAY IT DOWN SANCTUS REAL
MERCY (RADIO VERSION) MATT REDMAN
LIFT MY LIFE UP UNSPOKEN
WORDS HAWK NELSON (FEAT. BART MILLARD)
AMERICAN NOISE SKILLET
READY SET GO ROYAL TAILOR (FEAT. CAPITAL KINGS)

WORD MUSIC
& CHURCH RESOURCES

wordmusic.com

WOW HITS 2015

CONTENTS

We Believe

Recorded by NEWSBOYS

Words and Music by
MATTHEW HOOPER, RICHIE FIKE
and TRAVIS RYAN

Slowly, deliberately ♩ = 66

In this time ___ of des - per - a - tion,

when all we know ___ is doubt and ___ fear,

there is on - ly one ___ Foun - da - tion. We be - lieve. ___

The Only Name (Yours Will Be)

Recorded by BIG DADDY WEAVE

Words and Music by
BENJI COWART

12
1.
(to ms. 5)
2.
mf
2. Yours will be
And Yours is the name, the name
E2
mf (building slightly on D.S.)
15
that has saved me, mer - cy and grace, the pow'r that for - gave me. And Your
F♯
B
G♯m7
18
love is all I've ev - er need - ed.
E2
F♯
B
21
f
When I wake up in the land of glo - ry and
B2
f

Oceans (Where Feet May Fail)

Recorded by UNITED

**Words and Music by
JOEL HOUSTON, MATT CROCKER
and SALOMON LIGTHELM**

Slowly, worshipfully ♩ = 64

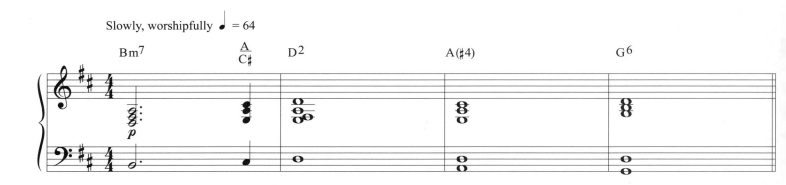

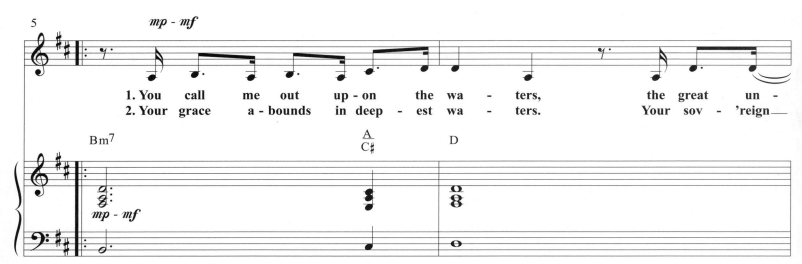

1. You call me out up-on the wa - ters, the great un -
2. Your grace a - bounds in deep - est wa - ters. Your sov - 'reign

2nd time: more motion (left hand - eighth note pulse)

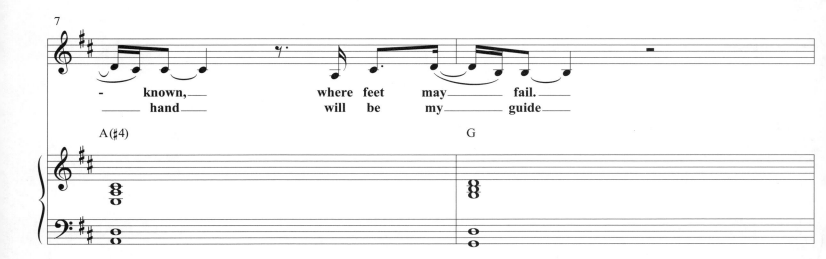

- known, where feet may fail.
— hand will be my guide

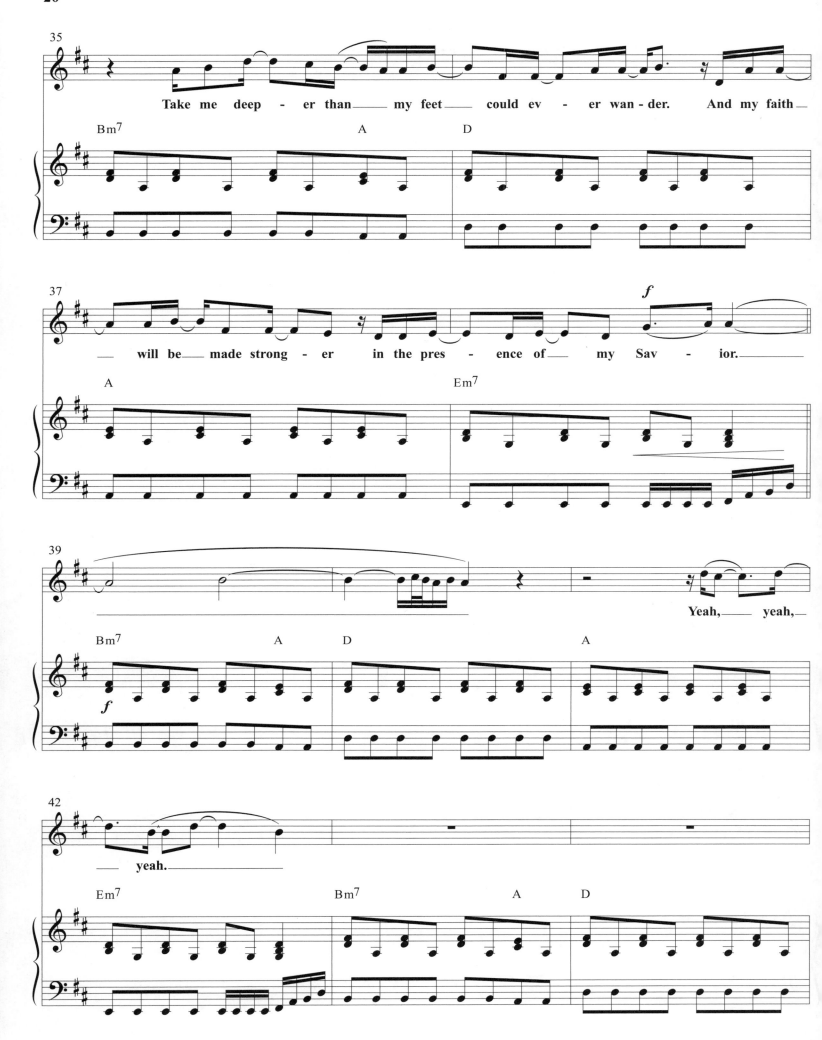

Thrive

Recorded by CASTING CROWNS

Words and Music by
MATTHEW WEST and MARK HALL

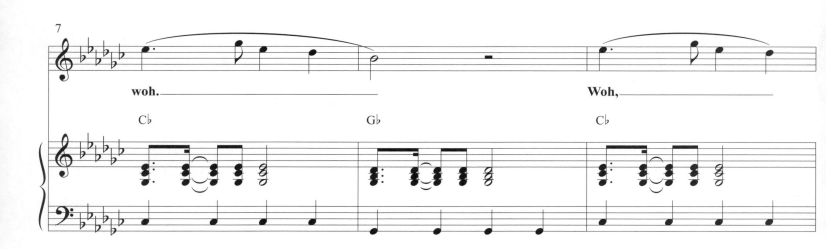

Do Something

Recorded by MATTHEW WEST

Words and Music by
MATTHEW WEST

Moderately ♩ = 112

I woke up— this morn-ing,— saw a world full of trou-ble now,— and thought,

"How'd we ev-er get so far down? And how's it ev-er gon-na turn a-round?"— So I

do some-thing."

Well, I don't know a-bout___ you,

but I'm___ sick and___ ti-red___ of life with___ no de-si-re.___ I

don't want a flame; I want a fi-re! I want to be___ the one___ who

D.S. al CODA
(to ms. 25)

stands up___ and says, "I'm___ gon-na do some-thing!"

70
sub. mp
still, no. If not us, then
E
sub. mp
73
f
who, if not me and you? Right
76
now, it's time for us to do some - thing.
A
f
Esus
E
79
If not now then when

Back to You

Recorded by MANDISA

Words and Music by
ALAN POWELL, BEN GLOVER
and DAVID GARCIA

2nd time to Coda ⊕
(*to ms. 41*)

Keep Making Me

Recorded by SIDEWALK PROPHETS

**Words and Music by
BEN MCDONALD, DAVID FREY
and SAM MIZELL**

I Am

Recorded by CROWDER

Words and Music by
DAVID CROWDER and ED CASH

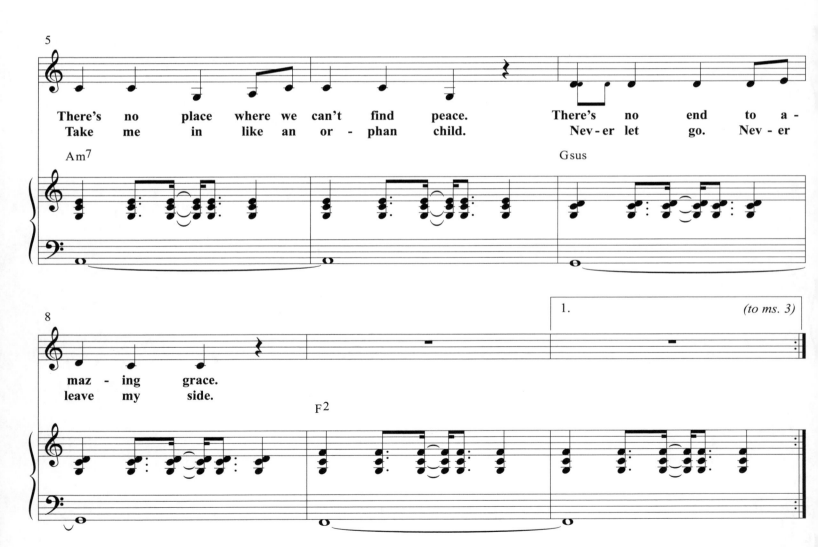

1. There's no space that His love can't reach.
2. Take me in with Your arms spread wide.

There's no place where we can't find peace.
Take me in like an or-phan child.

There's no end to a-maz-ing grace.
Nev-er let go. Nev-er leave my side.

Waterfall
Recorded by CHRIS TOMLIN

Words and Music by
CHRIS TOMLIN and ED CASH

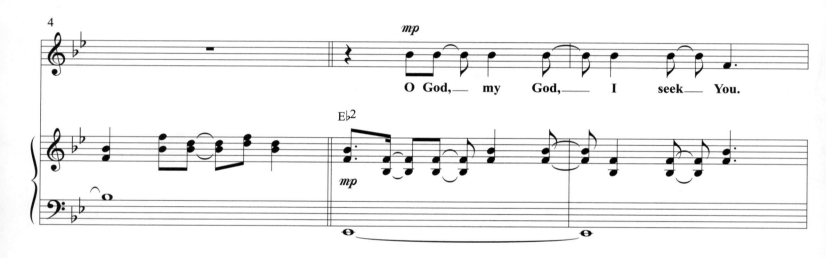

All the People Said Amen

Recorded by MATT MAHER

Words and Music by
**MATT MAHER, PAUL MOAK
and TREVOR MORGAN**

(Track begins with 2 bars percussion.)

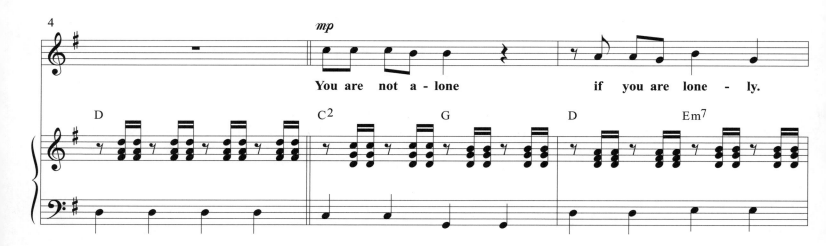

You are not a-lone   if you are lone - ly.

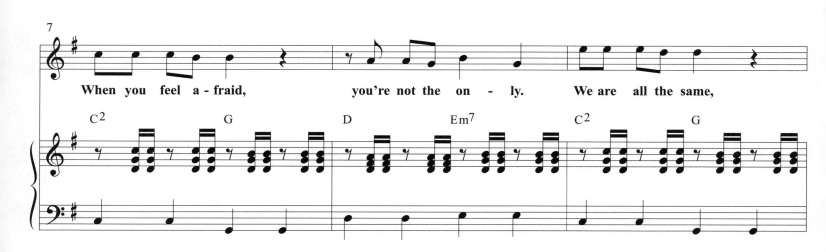

When you feel a-fraid,   you're not the on - ly.   We are   all the same,

Shake
Recorded by MERCYME

Words and Music by
**BARRY GRAUL, BART MILLARD,
BEN GLOVER, DAVID GARCIA,
MIKE SCHEUCHZER, NATHAN COCHRAN,
ROBBY SHAFFER and SOLOMON OLDS**

You Won't Let Go

Recorded by MICHAEL W. SMITH

**Words and Music by
MICHAEL W. SMITH, MIA FIELDES
and SETH MOSLEY**

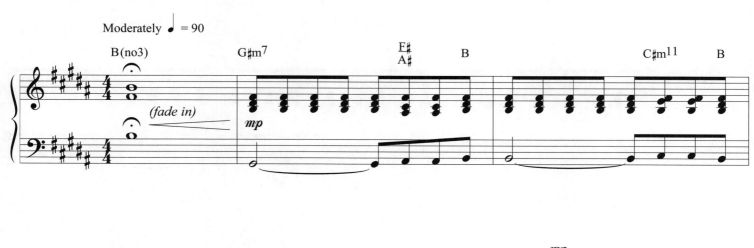

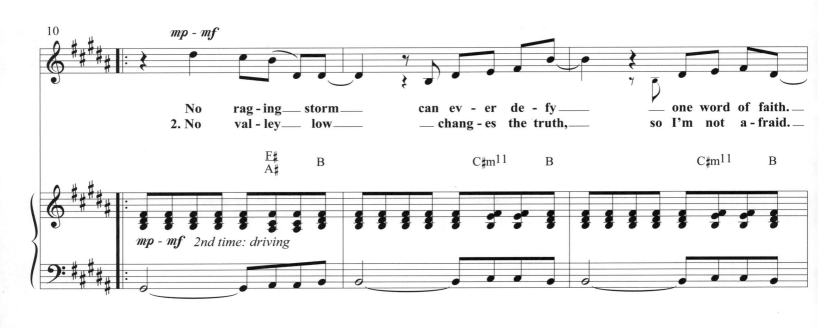

My Heart Is Yours

Recorded by PASSION
(featuring KRISTIAN STANFILL)

Words and Music by
KRISTIAN STANFILL, BRETT YOUNKER,
DANIEL CARSON, JASON INGRAM,
JUDSON WHEELER VAN DEVENTER
and WINFIELD SCOTT WEEDEN

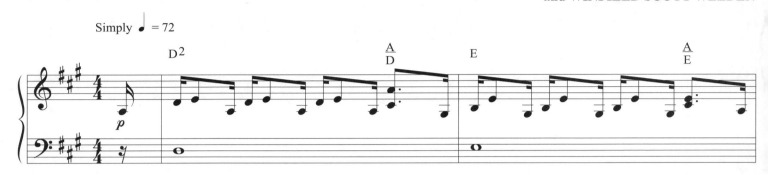

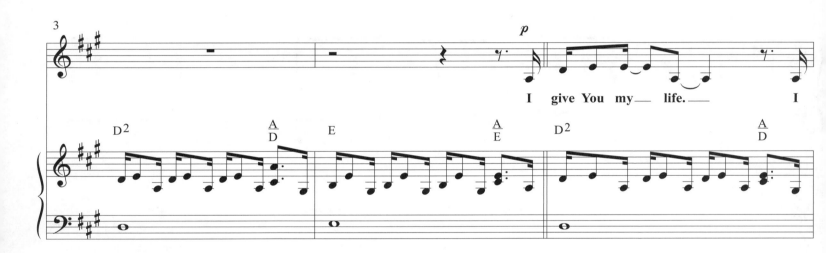

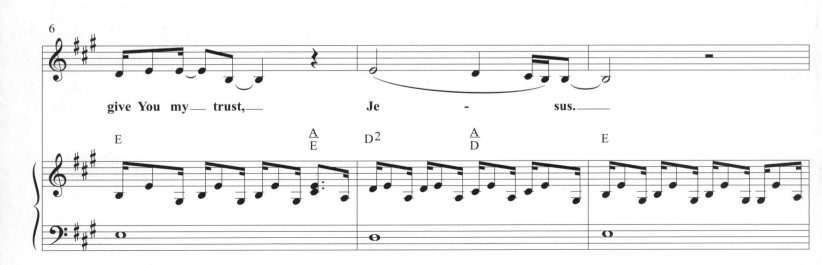

Glorious Unfolding

Recorded by STEVEN CURTIS CHAPMAN

Words and Music by
STEVEN CURTIS CHAPMAN

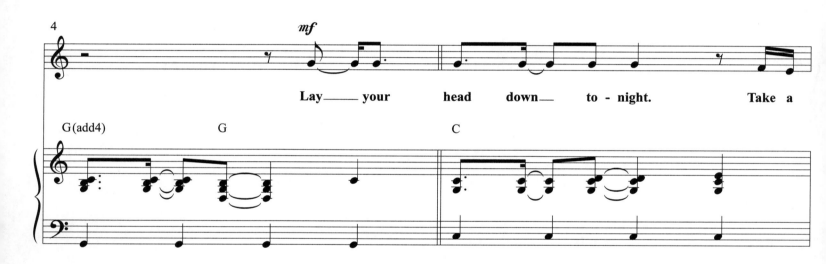

Lay___ your head down___ to-night. Take a

rest from___ the fight.___ Don't___ try to fig-ure it out.___

Forever (We Sing Hallelujah)

Recorded by KARI JOBE

Words and Music by
KARI JOBE, BRIAN JOHNSON,
CHRISTA BLACK GIFFORD, GABRIEL WILSON,
JENN JOHNSON and JOEL TAYLOR

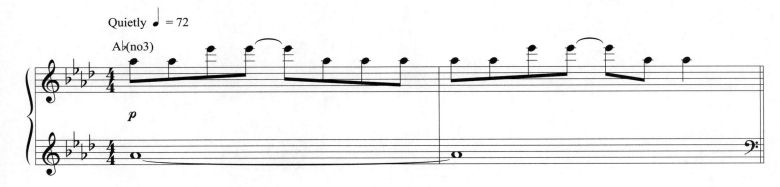

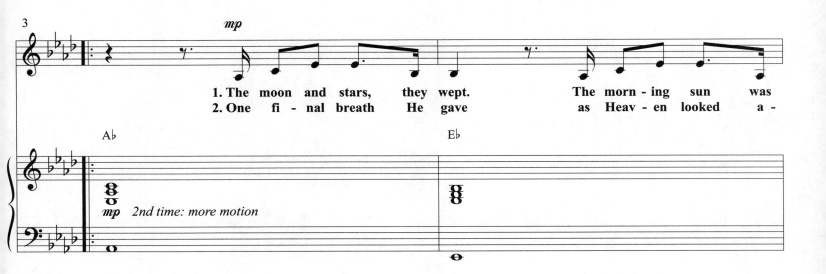

1. The moon and stars, they wept. The morn - ing sun was
2. One fi - nal breath He gave as Heav - en looked a -

dead. The Sav - ior of the world was fall - en.
way. The Son of God was laid in dark - ness.

I Will Follow

Recorded by JON GUERRA

Words and Music by
JON GUERRA and JACOB SOOTER

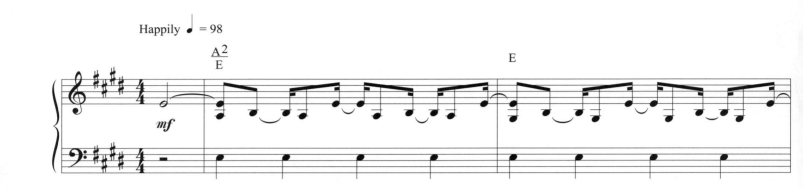

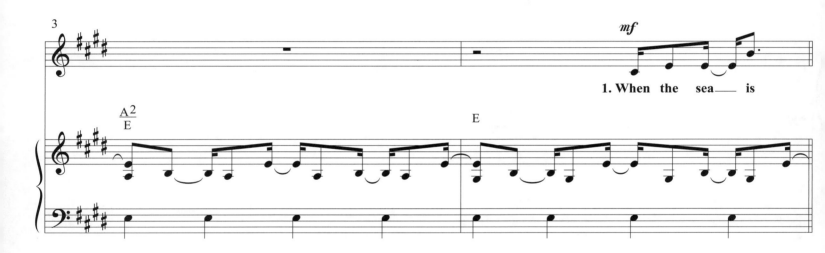

Beautiful

Recorded by DAN BREMNES

Words and Music by
**DAN BREMNES, BEN GLOVER,
DAVID ARTHUR GARCIA,
ED CASH and SCOTT CASH**

This Is Amazing Grace

Recorded by PHIL WICKHAM

Words and Music by
JEREMY RIDDLE, JOSH FARRO
and PHIL WICKHAM

133

Fix My Eyes

Recorded by FOR KING & COUNTRY

Words and Music by
JOEL SMALLBONE, LUKE SMALLBONE
and SETH MOSLEY

(Track begins with 2 bars percussion.)

Speak Life

Recorded by TOBY MAC

**Words and Music by
TOBY MCKEEHAN, JAMIE MOORE
and RYAN STEVENSON**

Beautiful Day

Recorded by JAMIE GRACE

**Words and Music by
JAMIE GRACE HARPER, CHRIS STEVENS,
MORGAN NICHOLS and TOBY MCKEEHAN**

Multiplied

Recorded by NEED TO BREATHE

**Words and Music by
BO RINEHART and
BEAR RINEHART**

158

More of You

Recorded by COLTON DIXON

Words and Music by
**BEN GLOVER, COLTON DIXON
and DAVID ARTHUR GARCIA**

Write Your Story

Recorded by FRANCESCA BATTISTELLI

Words and Music by
**FRANCESCA BATTISTELLI,
BEN GLOVER and DAVID GARCIA**

Detached, lightly ♩ = 94

No Man Is an Island

Recorded by TENTH AVENUE NORTH

Words and Music by
BRENDON SHIRLEY, JASON JAMISON,
JEFF OWEN, MIKE DONEHEY
and RUBEN JUAREZ

Press On

Recorded by BUILDING 429
(feat. BLANCA CALLAHAN)

Words and Music by
JASON ROY and ROB HAWKINS

(*Track begins with 2 bars percussion.*)

Some - times this world starts—— break - ing me down.——

I get so lost I think I'll nev - er be found.——

Come Alive

Recorded by JEREMY CAMP

Words and Music by
ANDY DODD and JEREMY CAMP

Lyrics: As I watch the world be-ing held cap-tive by dreams— that will nev - er be ful-filled in this life,

Alive
Recorded by YOUNG & FREE

**Words and Music by
ALEXANDER PAPPAS
and AODHAN KING**

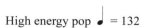

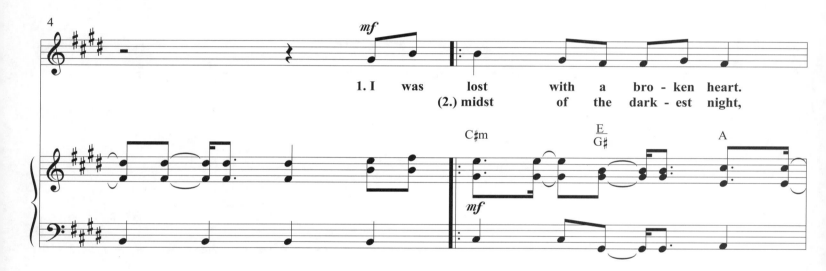

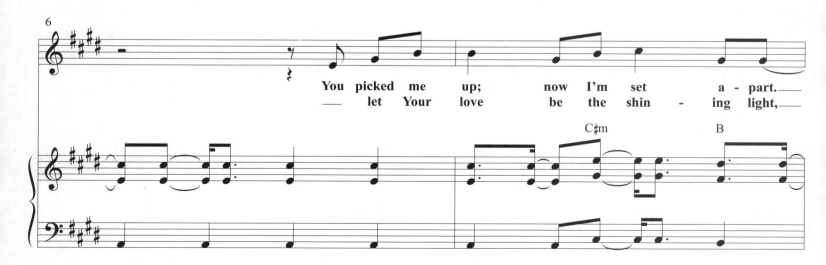

Love Alone Is Worth the Fight

Recorded by SWITCHFOOT

**Words and Music by
JON FOREMAN, TIM FOREMAN
and MIKE ELIZONDO**

210

Don't Deserve You

Recorded by PLUMB

Words and Music by
MATT BRONLEEWE and
TIFFANY ARBUCKLE LEE

Your Love Is Like a River

Recorded by THIRD DAY

Words and Music by
DAVID CARR, MAC POWELL,
MARK D. LEE and TAI ANDERSON

He Is With Us

Recorded by LOVE & THE OUTCOME

Words and Music by
JODI KING, CHRIS RADEMAKER
and SETH MOSLEY

Satisfied

Recorded by ABOUT A MILE

Words and Music by
ADAM KLUTINOTY, CASEY BROWN
and JONATHAN LINDLEY SMITH